Making Disney Scrapbook Pages

published by:

HOT OFF THE PRESS INC.

For a color catalog of nearly 750 products, send $2.00 to:

HOT OFF THE PRESS INC.
1250 N.W. Third, Dept. B
Canby, Oregon 97013
phone (503) 266-9102
fax (503) 266-8749
http://www.paperpizazz.com

At Hot Off The Press, we love Disney! We're also crazy about scrapbooking. Yet the idea for this book belongs to the talented women listed below. They're our in-house scrapbook specialists. They huddled, they plotted, and they designed nearly half of this book before bringing it to me as a concept. (I may be the president, but these women were determined and on a mission!) They **knew** customers would love a "big" book with Paper Pizazz™ sheets **and** cutouts **and** instructions focused on the Disney theme.

The folks at Disney Licensed Publishing loved the idea and quickly gave their blessing. LeNae, Susan, Shauna and Becky went back to their papers, scissors, glue and punches dedicated to creating a unique book showcasing wonderful things to do with Disney papers and personal photos. Some of these techniques take a little while to recreate and every one is worth the effort. So thank you, ladies for your vision, determination and talent in sharing some of the magic of Disney with the rest of us.

We would like to thank the page designers who contributed their magical ideas and wonderful page designs to this book. In alphabetical order they are:

- Shauna Berglund-Immel
- Susan Cobb
- LeNae Gerig
- Becky Goughnour

Hot Off The Press Production Credits

President: Paulette Jarvey
Vice-President: Teresa Nelson
Production Manager: Tom Muir
Project Editor: Kris Andrews
Editor: Lynda Hill
Graphic Designers: Jacie Pete, Carlee Justis
Photographer: John McNally
Digital Imagers: Victoria Gleason, Larry Seith

Making Disney Scrapbook Pages

- 68 sample album pages
- 14 techniques
- 40 sheets of Paper Pizazz™
  (*a $19.60 value*)

TABLE OF CONTENTS

Designing the Pages

Your hands are holding a very special book. In fact, it's quite unique! Our scrapbook specialists have captured the magic of Disney and have shown us how to sprinkle it throughout any scrapbook. Everything is here at your fingertips—page layout ideas, Paper Pizazz™ sheets, cutouts, full-size patterns and ideas for even more album pages.

As you'll see from the page ideas, you don't need photos of Disneyland or Walt Disney World to make these album pages. Nor do you need to have photos of people wearing Disney garments. Your photos, your simple everyday photos, are perfect for these album pages. What you do need is a sense of fun and an eye for the magical.

While most of the page ideas shown use the Paper Pizazz™ sheets bound in this book, most of the papers originally came from existing Paper Pizazz™ books. Next to each album page is a list of materials used to create that page. If "*New*" appears after the Paper Pizazz™ listing, that means the sheet is in this book. The titles of the book or the page kit the sheet was originally published in follows the word "*New*". So when you need more Disney Paper Pizazz™ sheets, you can get them!

There are, however, six Paper Pizazz™ sheets that exist only in this book. They are: bouncing Tigger (used in a design at the bottom of page 22), Pooh faces (shown at the bottom of page 23), fall leaves Piglet (shown at the bottom of page 32), Pooh's favorite things (used at the top of page 33), Mickey silhouette on red (used on a page at the bottom of page 34) and blue Mickey tiles (shown at the top of page 35). Remember, too, when using the cutouts in this book, to cut each out with a narrow white border to be sure your cutout will show up on the patterned paper.

So figuratively (or literally), let's put on our Mouse ears and begin scrapbooking!

Good Question...We've Got an Answer!

Q. What is the difference between a "cutout" and a Punch-Out™?

A. Cutouts are included in this book and you must cut them out yourself. Punch-Outs™ are perforated images that are purchased separately in themed books. While you cut out the image as closely or with as wide a border as you like from this book, Punch-Outs™ are designed with a narrow white border around each image. We've found by adding a thin white mat around the image it "pops" off the page gaining attention. When matted on a solid color paper, a very quick double-mat effect is achieved.

This book uses the following Punch-Outs™: *Pooh ABC Punch-Outs™*, *Mickey & Friends Punch-Outs™* and *Pooh Punch-Outs™*. All are Paper Pizazz™ made by Hot Off The Press. Both cutouts and Punch-Outs™ are used in this book—sometimes on the same album page! It's okay to substitute Punch-Outs™ for cutouts.

Q. I love your Disney papers, but I find some a little too busy for my tastes. What can I do?

A. If you're nervous about using a full sheet of patterned paper with your photos try cutting the paper into strips, squares or letters (see page 18). This is also an excellent way to stretch one page into two or more album pages. Don't forget "The Golden Rule of patterned paper" whenever you use patterned paper, mat your photos with solid paper to make the photo pop off the page.

Q. I have never been to Disneyland or Walt Disney World® and I don't have any Disney pictures. Can I still do the pages in the book?

A. All you really need to do these pages is to have an appreciation for the Disney characters. If you don't have photos of family at a Disney theme park or dressed in Disney clothing try using zoo pictures on *The Jungle Book* page or swimming photos on a *The Little Mermaid* page. Baby photos are great for Pooh pages...and so are adult photos!

Q. There is a cute Pooh page in this book, but I'd like to do a Mickey page. How can I do the same layout?

A. Substituting characters on a page is easy. Choose a substitute paper with a design that can be cut apart horizontally or vertically as done in the original design you are re-creating. Once you have chosen the appropriate paper the layout can be copied easily. Here, we substituted Mickey paper for Ari's first day of school instead of the Pooh paper used at the top of page 14.

8 Steps for Building a Magical Page

1 Select your photos based on the theme or event for your album page. You might think of each scrapbook page as illustrating a story.

2 Select Disney patterned paper to complement your photos or to emphasize the theme or event for your album page. A whimsical patterned Disney paper may perfectly mirror the story, mood or personality of the people in your photos. The paper colors can also coordinate or match the clothing or background colors in your photos.

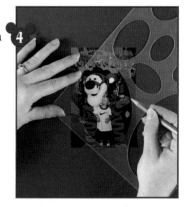

3 Choose solid colored papers that coordinate with both your photos and your Disney themed paper.

4 Crop your photos. Use plastic templates to crop the perfect size and shape for the page.

5 Another fun alternative is to silhouette-cut the image(s) in the photo. Silhouetting means to cut very closely around the person or object. This allows the focal point of the photo to really stand out and you can place it in fun and interesting environments! This technique looks best when used with entire shapes like cars or bodies that won't get lost on the page.

6 Mat your cropped photos with plain colored paper and cut a 1/16"-1/2" wide border. Use straight-edged or decorative-edged scissors. Mix and match cuts, double-mat or mix shapes and sizes. Silhouette-cut photos can be matted, too.

7 Arrange the photos on the background paper. Establish a focal point, vary the photo sizes and shapes, overlap the elements and fill the center, as illustrated in the many magical layouts in this book.

8 Add decorative elements such as Punch-Outs™, cutouts, punches, stickers and die cuts that complement and coordinate with the paper, photos and theme. Write (or journal) the story represented by your photos. Journal on a mat, border or a shape cut from solid color paper. Mat the journal shapes as shown, if desired, and glue it to the page.

Hints and Tips for Disney Scrapbooking

 What's the easiest way to transfer patterns from this book?

Trace the entire pattern including all of the detail lines onto tracing paper (see page 11). Lay the traced pattern on solid-color or patterned paper. Hold or tape the pattern on one edge and slip a piece of transfer paper, shiny side down, between the traced pattern and the paper. Use dark transfer paper when transferring lines onto light-color papers and use white transfer paper when transferring lines onto dark-color papers. Draw over the character outlines with a pencil. (You will use the same pattern to transfer the face and detail lines after the character has been assembled.) Remove the tracing and transfer papers and draw over the transferred lines using an acid-free pen in a color that shows up well (a black pen for light papers, a white pen for dark papers).

 What kind of glue or adhesive is best to use in my scrapbook page designs?

We used repositionable glue because it allows us to assemble designs directly onto a page without being committed to the placement. Then you can change your mind until it's perfect! Apply the glue to the back of the paper and let it dry. Then, when you are satisfied with where you have placed it, you can use permanent glue to affix your elements to the page.

Photo mounting tapes are very useful when you really want to anchor an object to the page. For example, when making projects in the "moveable parts" and "flaps, doors & windows" sections, the pull tabs adhere much more securely when reinforced with photo mounting tapes.

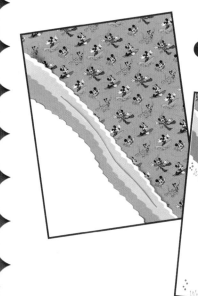

What's the best order to work in when designing a Paper Piecing or Movable Parts scrapbook page?

When making special elements such as moveable part mechanisms or pieced paper characters, it's best to complete the moveable element first and then mat and place the photos in the space remaining. Take the Mickey Water Slide page shown at the bottom of page 33 for example. Construct the slide and the moveable Mickey and glue it along the page left. Then mat and position the photos in the upper page right. When paper piecing, it's easiest to complete the character first, then mat the photos. Afterwards, arrange all of the elements as you would plan out the placement with a die cut or Punch-Out™.

7 Tips for Paper Piecing

1 **Using tracing paper:** Lay tracing paper over the selected pattern in this book and trace all of the lines with a pencil. This is the master pattern.

2 **Using transfer paper:** Lay the master pattern over the selected patterned or solid color paper. Slip the transfer paper (shiny side down) in between the master pattern and the selected patterned or solid-color paper. Draw over the lines of the master pattern. Transfer each individual shape of the master pattern onto the selected patterned or solid color paper. Cut out each along the lines.

3 Many of the Disney characters are outlined in black. Mat each piece on black paper and cut each out. Or simply outline each with an acid-free black permanent pen. A mat adds a physical depth and texture to each character piece that a drawn outline doesn't provide.

4 Use repositionable glue as you assemble the design onto the final mat paper. Put all the layers together and make sure everything fits before gluing anything down permanently. Sometimes it's helpful to lay the original character pattern over the pieces to ensure proper placement. Cut around the entire character on the final mat paper.

5 Lay the master pattern over the pieced character. Slip transfer paper between the layers (see step 2) and draw over the detail lines, transferring them to the pieced character.

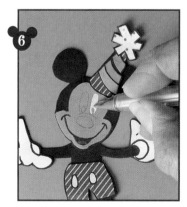

6 Remove the paper and pattern and draw over the transferred lines with an acid-free black permanent pen. Use opaque pens to fill in the eyes and mouths rather than cutting out these small pieces from colored paper.

7 Glue the pieced character to the album page and give yourself a pat on the back!

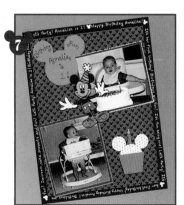

Use 8½"x11" Papers to Create 12"x12" Page Designs

The patterned papers included in this book are 8½"x11". We know many of us like the 12"x12" format, too! So we've included lots of examples of these larger page designs throughout this book.

Don't limit yourself to mounting a sheet of 8½"x11" paper on a plain 12"x12" sheet of paper! Consider using a patterned sheet for the background and these great papers as elements of your design.

With Mickey officiating, Cori and Matt were engaged at Disneyland. A crowd gathered to watch the festivities and cheered when Cori said "yes!" to the Big Question.

You've found an element that fits your theme perfectly, but it's in an 8½"x11" paper and you design 12"x12" pages! Cut the element, like the castle shown here, from the paper and glue it to a patterned 12"x12" background sheet. Then mat and place your photos around the element. The blue stars background paper echoes the theme of the page, too!

Paper Pizazz™: Castle (*New, Magic Kingdom Papers*), blue stars (*Birthday Time!*)
Solid Paper Pizazz™: pink, blue, yellow (*Plain Pastels*)
Cutouts: Mickey, Minnie (*New, Magic Kingdom Papers*)
Knife: X-acto®
Black Pens: Zig® Writer and Calligraphy by EK Success, Ltd.
Page designer: Becky Goughnour

A patterned background can create the theme of your page design. The 12"x12" moiré patterned background provides a soft pink backdrop of shimmering lines like the reflection in a mirror. The Seven Dwarfs paper enforces the page theme. Of course, you don't want to cover up the pattern. Cut the chosen 8½"x11" patterned paper diagonally from corner to corner! This provides two large triangle pieces to add as design elements to your 12"x12" page. The mirror shape (pattern on page 39) reflects the theme, and cutouts tie it together. Add circle and diamond punches for a bejeweled look.

Paper Pizazz™: Seven Dwarfs (*Disney Classics #2*), pink moiré (*Our Wedding Day*)
Solid Paper Pizazz™: white, yellow, pink, lavender (*Plain Pastels*)
Cutouts: Snow White, Dopey (*New*)
Circle and diamond punches: Family Treasures™
Decorative scissors: Imperial by Fiskars®
Black pen: Zig® Writer by EK Success, Ltd.
Page designer: LeNae Gerig

Choose a 12"x12" pattern that coordinates with the 8½"x11" pattern. Here, the black border around each Eeyore block is continued by mounting the full sheet on a dark patterned 12"x12" paper. Placing the sheet on one side leaves a wide strip for fun lettering. Use coordinating alphabet Punch-Outs™ to write the name in fun Disney letters. Groups of dots and spiraling squiggles embellish the letters and repeat the action of Eeyore's somersaulting.

Paper Pizazz™: Eeyore blocks *(New, Just You and Pooh)*, black with blue dots *(Bold & Bright)*
Solid Paper Pizazz™: lavender *(Plain Pastels)*, black *(Solid Jewel Tones)*
Punch-Outs™: letters *(Pooh ABC)*
Pens: lavender, light blue Milky Gel Roller by Pentel
Page designer: LeNae Gerig

A subtle patterned 12"x12" background can add more color to your page design without any fear of overwhelming your photo. Cut the 8½"x11" patterned paper into strips to space the pattern farther apart on your 12"x12" page. Cut two 1⅝"x11" strips, two 1¾"x5" strips and one 5"x5½" piece. Mat all of the pieces on blue paper and arrange on the 12"x12" sheet of paper as shown. Mat your photo; then trace and cut letters from yellow to add some color contrast to your page. Off-setting the photo will draw the viewer's eye right to it.

Paper Pizazz™: E is for Eeyore *(New, Winnie the Pooh and Baby, Too!)*, purple and lavender *(Great Backgrounds)*
Solid Paper Pizazz™: blue, yellow *(Plain Pastels)*
Alphabet template: Fat Caps by Frances Meyer, Inc.®
Blue pen: Zig® Writer by EK Success, Ltd.
Page designer: LeNae Gerig

Create a Two-Page Spread (or More!) with One Sheet of Pizazz™

Only have one sheet of patterned paper and need more for a two- or three-page spread? Here are a few great examples of how to make the most out of that one sheet. Cut it into squares or strips. Or mat your photos on the sheet of patterned paper. Split the sheet and use half of it on each side of a two-page spread. Or cut out elements in the patterned design and use them as cutouts on your page. Lots of choices!

Share a single sheet of paper by splitting it into two pieces. Use two matching solid sheets to create the spread; then glue one piece of patterned paper to the far left and the other to the far right side of the spread. Cut your photos into lots of shapes and mat them on bright colors. Embellish the solid paper with small and large drawn dots–and use several great Punch-Outs™ to continue the confetti theme of the patterned paper.

Paper Pizazz™: Pooh confetti border *(New, School Days with Pooh)*
Solid Paper Pizazz™: aqua blue, green, blue, goldenrod, fuchsia *(Plain Brights)*
Punch-Outs™: faces *(Pooh)*
Decorative scissors: Ripple by Fiskars®
Black pen: Zig® Writer by EK Success, Ltd.
Page designer: LeNae Gerig

Cut the elements of one patterned paper sheet to use throughout a two page spread! Cut the blocks from the patterned paper and mat each one. Use the pen to make stitch lines on and between each block to make the quilt theme. Glue the new quilt blocks evenly spaced around the outer edges of two pieces of yellow paper. Embellish the blocks with buttons made from small circle punches and glue them at each corner. Punch large circle buttons, draw circles for button holes and glue them among the photos continuing the baby quilt theme.

Paper Pizazz™: Pooh quilt *(New, Winnie the Pooh and Baby, Too!)*
Solid Paper Pizazz™: yellow, pink, blue, green *(Plain Pastels)*
Small and large circle punches: Family Treasures™
Decorative scissors: Ripple by Fiskars®
Black pen: Zig® Writer by EK Success, Ltd.
Page designer: LeNae Gerig

Cut strips that span two pages to unify the spread and continue the theme. Cut patterned paper into thick and thin strips following the paper design. Glue the strips to span the spread pages as shown. Silhouette a photo for each page. Mat the remaining photos using color-coordinated papers. Pooh's face is easy to trace onto die cut shapes (pattern on page 39) and adds a surprise to both Christopher's and Molly's pages.

Paper Pizazz™: Pooh Halloween *(New, Special Days with Pooh)*
Solid Paper Pizazz™: yellow *(Plain Pastels)*, light and dark orange *(Plain Brights)*, black *(Solid Jewel Tones)*
Die cuts: bat, pumpkin by Accu/Cut® Systems, Inc.
Decorative scissors: Deckle by Family Treasures™
White pen: Milky Gel Roller by Pentel
Pens: black, green, red Zig® Writer by EK Success, Ltd.
Page designer: LeNae Gerig

This sort of "repeating-pattern" paper really lends itself well to this technique. The design allows you to easily cut the elements (here, the face stamps) into strips, frames or single images to scatter throughout two, three or even more pages. This helps create unity and cohesion among a multiple page spread.

Cut six strips from the bottom of the patterned paper and glue one to the top and bottom of each piece of background paper. Use the remaining paper to make a frame by simply cutting the center from a rectangle. Or glue strips to the top and bottom of a photo as a border. Cut any remaining images from the paper, glue to colorful circle mat papers and glue randomly.

Paper Pizazz™: Mickey and Friends Faces *(New, Playtime with Mickey and Friends)*, black with dots *(Bright Great Backgrounds, also available in bulk)*
Solid Paper Pizazz™: Red, yellow, aqua blue *(Plain Brights)*
Large circle punch: Family Treasures™
Decorative scissors: Ripply by McGill, Inc.
Black Pen: Zig® Writer by EK Success, Ltd.
Page designer: LeNae Gerig

Pull Elements From the Background to Embellish a Page

A great way to be sure all the elements coordinate is to borrow an idea from the background paper. Allow a predominant color in the paper to inspire your choice; then pick a shape to help you make your choice. Finally, choose stickers, Punch-Outs™ or die cuts that repeat the design to provide a beautifully synchronized album page!

Not only are the red flowers a great place to journal, but they are also taken right from the background paper! The cute flower on Minnie's hat is brought to the foreground of the page with these great shapes. They're easy to make, too. Use a circle template to draw 1¼" wide yellow circle centers and 2" wide red circle petals. Cut around the circles just outside the line. Overlap the petals gluing a center to the middle and glue to the page overlapping photos. Trim any extending flowers even with the page.

Paper Pizazz™: classic Minnie *(Mickey & The Old Gang)*
Solid Paper Pizazz™: red, goldenrod *(Plain Brights)*, black *(Solid Jewel Tones)*
Black pen: Zig® Writer by EK Success, Ltd.
Page Designer: LeNae Gerig

If you don't have a Punch-Out™ or die cut to match your page theme or patterned paper design, try making your own using punches! Punch the flowers from salmon, blue and yellow papers. Use the pattern to draw the detail lines on each flower and leaf. Glue a ¼" yellow punched circle to the center of each flower. Crop each photo into an oval and glue a flower with a leaf on each side around the oval to frame it.

Paper Pizazz™: giggling Thumper *(New, Disney Classics)*
Solid Paper Pizazz™: salmon, blue, yellow, green, white, ivory, lavender *(Plain Pastels)*
Flower, leaf and ¼" circle punches: McGill, Inc.
Pens: black, green Zig® Writer by EK Success, Ltd.
Page Designer: Shauna Berglund-Immel

The large hands on this page not only mirror the action in the photo, but they also copy Mickey's hands shown in the background paper! This makes for a fun and whimsical page that is also very quick and easy to do.

Trim ¼" from all sides of the patterned paper and mat it on black to border the page like each square in the patterned paper. Mat a photo on contrasting yellow. Write "I Love You This Much!" on a 1¾"x2¼" piece of white paper. Mat it on black then yellow. Draw squiggles and dots around the border of the journaling and the bordering black frame to mimic the lines around each square in the pattern. Trace two "Mickey Hands" (pattern on page 40) onto white paper and cut them out. Draw around each hand and glue the pieces to the page as shown. There are lots of elements from the background paper used in this page.

Paper Pizazz™: Mickey's picnic (*Mickey & The Old Gang*)
Solid Paper Pizazz™: yellow, white (*Plain Pastels*), black (*Solid Jewel Tones*)
Black pen: Zig® Writer by EK Success, Ltd.
White pen: Milky Gel Roller by Pentel
Page Designer: LeNae Gerig

Pulling the elements from the background paper allows you to continue the fun theme of the paper into a larger 12"x12" format, too! The circus balls—exactly like the ones in the patterned paper— create a unique and fun border around this page. Punch a small blue, red and green circle. Cut a ¼" wide strip from the center of the blue circle, mat it on red, and glue on the green circle. Mat the ball on blue. Punch yellow stars and glue two to the center of each ball. Repeat to make many balls and glue them among your journaled border. Scissor edges can also echo elements of the patterned paper as does the scalloped red mat with the stars.

Paper Pizazz™: circus Dumbo (*New, Disney Classics*)
Solid Paper Pizazz™: yellow, white (*Solid Pastel Papers*), red, aqua blue, neon green (*Plain Brights*)
Cutout: Dumbo (*New, Disney Classics*)
Small circle and star punches: Marvy® Uchida
Decorative scissors: Spindle and Scallop by Fiskars®
Pens: green, yellow, blue Milky Gel Roller by Pentel
Green pen: Zig® Writer by EK Success, Ltd.
Page designer: Shauna Berglund-Immel

Split a Page for More Pizazz

There are lots of ways to use a piece of Disney patterned paper! Splitting the page is yet another great way to add a bit of magical pizazz to your album. It can add dimension to your album page or help the patterned paper feel less overwhelming if you're still feeling cautious about using it in your designs. Splitting an 8½"x11" sheet of patterned paper works well when you want to use it in a 12"x12" page design. It also helps stretch a single sheet of patterned paper over several album pages. There are many examples of splitting a page throughout this book—here are two more!

Add dimension to a page with multiple mats creating a textured "stage" that features a favorite photo. Splitting the page breaks up the pattern making it feel less busy while still bringing that adorable Disney look.

Cut the patterned paper into an 8" square. Cut the square into 1" wide diagonal strips. Line up the heads when you glue the strips to black paper so Mickey's face remains a continuous image. Then trim the jagged edges of the square to 6½"x7". Mat it on goldenrod, then again on black and glue it to the center of the album page. Double mat a favorite photo and glue a ⅜" wide strip to border the top and bottom of the page.

Paper Pizazz™: Mickey rainbow (New, Mickey and Friends)
Solid Paper Pizazz™: red, blue, goldenrod (Plain Brights), black (Solid Jewel Tones)
White pen: Milky Gel Roller by Pentel
Page designer: LeNae Gerig

What a great way to split an 8½"x11" paper for a 12"x12" design! Cut the page into four 2" wide strips. Mat them on a bright paper and glue them evenly spaced across a 12"x12" paper. Foam mounting tape does a bubbly good job of creating depth in your design as shown with these matted bubble letters! Use a blue pen to draw a comma shaped highlight on each bubble.

Paper Pizazz™: Flounder (New, The Little Mermaid)
Solid Paper Pizazz™: white, light blue (Solid Pastel Papers), light orange, yellow, aqua blue (Plain Brights)
Cutout: Flounder (New, The Little Mermaid)
Large circle punch: Family Treasurers™
Alphabet Template: by Provo Craft
Foam mounting tape: Pop Dots™ by All Night Media, Inc.
Black pen: Zig® Millennium by EK Success, Ltd.
White pen: Milky Gel Roller by Pentel
Page designer: Shauna Berglund-Immel

Create a Photo Collage

A collage is a great way to get a ton of photos on one page. Collages may include many photos of one event or one person. Collage the various Christmas tree pictures you've taken over the years, or the annual pictures of your birthday cakes!

Combine those "little pictures"—the ones that don't really portray a special event but definitely capture the child's personality—into a "photomontage!"

Trace the pink Mickey head (pattern on page 40) onto black paper and cut it out. Trim two photos into circles ⅛" smaller than the ears. Glue them in place. Silhouette a variety of photos and glue them to overlap each other. Trim the piece into a circle ⅛" smaller than the head and glue it in place.

Paper Pizazz™: Mickey (*Mickey & The Old Gang*), red with white dots (*Ho Ho Ho!!!*)
Solid Paper Pizazz™: black (*Solid Jewel Tones*), white (*Plain Pastels*)
Alphabet template: Wacky Alphabet by Frances Meyer, Inc®
Black pen: Zig® Writer by EK Success, Ltd.
Page designer: LeNae Gerig

Silhouette-cut the photos (see page 9, step 4) then combine them all on a solid color paper as shown in the examples below.

Do you have lots of pictures of one event and want to include them all in your scrapbook? Try this collage technique. Silhouette each photo and then glue them all so that they overlap one another on a sheet of black paper. Glue Pooh Punch-Out™ characters among the silhouettes to peek around them. Cut the black paper ⅛" larger around the collage and glue to the center of patterned paper. This is effective regardless of what paper size you use! Embellish the page with matted Punch-Outs™, a journaling plaque and borders!

Paper Pizazz™: purple dots (*Bold & Bright*)
Solid Paper Pizazz™: black (*Solid Jewel Tones*)
Punch-Outs™: faces (*Pooh*)
White pen: Milky Gel Roller by Pentel
Page designer: LeNae Gerig

Build Brilliant Borders

Adding a border to your page design can make all the difference for your page! Cute Disney characters glued along the side, top or bottom of the page bring playful life to each page design.

There are no rules to making borders! Use punches, cutouts, Punch-Outs™ or even little photos as shown on the next page. A border can be linear or circular—they define focus and keep the eyes roaming around those favorite photos that you want to showcase!

Design a border that reinforces the theme of the page like this Christmas wreath of Disney pals! Crop a photo into a large circle and glue it to the center of a sheet of black paper. Overlap and glue theme-related Punch-Outs™ around the photo. Punch and tuck holly leaves and berries among them to create a wreath. Cut around the wreath leaving a ⅛" border. Then glue it to a patterned mat as shown. The signatures background paper names the characters on the Punch-Outs™!

Paper Pizazz™: signatures (*New, Mickey and Friends*), red with white dots (*Ho Ho Ho!!!*)
Solid Paper Pizazz™: black (*Solid Jewel Tones*), red, green (*Plain Brights*)
Punch-Outs™: Mickey and friends characters (*Mickey & Friends*)
Holly punch: Family Treasures™
¼" circle punch: McGill, Inc.
Black pen: Zig™ Millennium by EK Success, Ltd.
White pen: Milky Gel Roller by Pentel
Page designer: LeNae Gerig

Cut apart patterned paper into character blocks like these for an easy way to create a border! Mat each square and glue them along the page top and bottom. The ferns patterned paper background continues the jungle theme.

Think of all of the squares that one sheet of paper provides! A four page spread could easily be made using this border technique. If you don't have *Jungle Book* Disney photos, any zoo pictures or outdoor photos would be great on this page, too.

Paper Pizazz™: Jungle Book scenes (*New, Disney Classics*), ferns (*Great Outdoors, also available in bulk*)
Solid Paper Pizazz™: light green (*Plain Pastels*), blue (*Plain Brights*), black (*Solid Jewel Tones*)
Decorative Scissors: Deckle by Family Treasures™
Black pen: Zig® Writer by EK Success, Ltd.
Page designer: LeNae Gerig

This adorable 8½"x11" paper is designed with a border on the page—Kanga and Roo! Placed on a 12"x12" page, there's lots of space left for another border. Create it using small photos! Much like the matted character blocks border shown at the bottom of page 20, these blocks feature pictures of your own lil' Roo! Draw a loopy pen border in the open space. Cut the photos into squares and double mat each one. Glue them over the drawn border. Embellish with pen dots and small heart punches.

Paper Pizazz™: Kanga and Roo (*New, Pooh On the Edge*)
Solid Paper Pizazz™: dark pink, yellow, lavender, aqua blue (*Solid Pastel Papers*)
Small heart punch: Family Treasures™
Black pen: Zig® Writer by EK Success. Ltd.
Page designer: LeNae Gerig

While the matted Pooh and Piglet silhouette punches make a great page top border, the Peek-a-Boo Pooh at the page bottom is really an element cut from a patterned paper in this book! Cut Pooh from the paper and glue him to peek in from the bottom of a 12"x12" page. Cut 1¼" squares of black paper and punch the center of each with the silhouette punch. Mat each square on yellow. Glue the squares evenly spaced to the top of the page tilting each of them at different angles. Use the pen to draw a loopy line between each square. Draw black strings with bows around each matted photo and embellish the page with punched plaid hearts, black swirls and pen dots.

Paper Pizazz™: Pooh (*New, Peek-a-Boo Pooh*)
Plain Paper Pizazz™: light green, aqua blue, yellow (*Solid Pastel Papers*), black (*Solid Jewel Tones*)
Pooh and Piglet Silhouette Punch: All Night Media®, Inc.
Heart and swirl punches: Family Treasures™
Black pen: Zig® Millennium by EK Success, Ltd.
Page designer: LeNae Gerig

Embellish Pages With Line Art

Drawing your own accents with pens or markers can be a very satisfying expression of your creative side. And, really, it's not hard! Keep a loose grip on the pen and let your heart guide your hand. We'll let you in on a little secret—even our pros draw their line art in pencil first, and then go over the lines in pen when they're pleased with the design. After a few pages, you'll find that looping free-form squiggles, lines and dots is as simple as spelling M-I-C-K-E-Y!

Creating line art around a page makes for a unique way to fill empty spaces or when making a border. A white pen gives great contrast when used to draw bubbles on a dark background page. Continue the bubble theme with circle punched borders around the photo mats. Cut a slit in the sand at the bottom of the page and slip a matted photo behind it to create dimension in the design. Glue the cutouts to the page before drawing the border.

Paper Pizazz™: Ariel and Flounder (*New, The Little Mermaid*)
Solid Paper Pizazz™: blue, white, yellow (*Solid Pastel Papers*)
Cutouts: Ariel, Sebastian, border friends (*New, The Little Mermaid*)
Decorative scissors: Bubbles by Fiskars®
1/16" circle punch: McGill, Inc.
Knife: X-acto®
White pen: Milky Gel Roller by Pentel
Page designer: Shauna Berglund-Immel

Mat the photo first, then use the remaining patterned paper to cut letters and spell out a journal-border! Cut out the letters and glue them to border the page. Glue Tigger images to overlap the mat and embellish the letters and images with theme-related line art like these bouncing coils and motion lines.

Paper Pizazz™: bouncing Tigger (*New*), dots on yellow (*Stripes, Checks & Dots*)
Solid Paper Pizazz™: light pink (*Plain Pastels*)
Punch-Out™: Tigger bouncing on tail (*Pooh*)
Cutout: hopping Tigger (*New*)
1/16" circle punch: McGill, Inc.
Decorative scissor: Scallop by Fiskars®
Alphabet template: Fat Lower Case Alphabet by Frances Meyer, Inc.®
Black Pen: Zig® Writer by EK Success, Ltd.
Page designer: Shauna Berglund-Immel

Embellish the page with pen work to add creative details to your work. The patterned paper on this page was trimmed to 8"x10" in order to leave room for a wave border around the edges. Punch bubbles from solid color papers. A few of those shown are punched from blue Pooh signature patterned paper and provide a nice coordinating element with the pink Pooh signature patterned towel and the Punch-Outs™. Draw curved highlights on the bubbles to create dimension and layer them to fill the tub. Glue the towel to "drape" over the edge of the tub. (Bathtub and towel patterns are shown on page 41.)

Paper Pizazz™: pink and blue Pooh signature *(New)*, bubbles
    (Baby, also available in bulk)
Solid Paper Pizazz™: blue, light blue, lavender, white
    (Plain Pastels)
Punch-Outs™: Pooh, Tigger, Piglet, Eeyore *(Pooh)*
Small and medium circle punches: Family Treasures™
¼" circle punch: McGill, Inc.
Decorative scissors: Wave by Family Treasurers™
Black pen: Zig® Writer by EK Success, Ltd.
Page Designer: LeNae Gerig

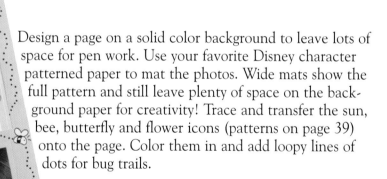

Design a page on a solid color background to leave lots of space for pen work. Use your favorite Disney character patterned paper to mat the photos. Wide mats show the full pattern and still leave plenty of space on the background paper for creativity! Trace and transfer the sun, bee, butterfly and flower icons (patterns on page 39) onto the page. Color them in and add loopy lines of dots for bug trails.

Paper Pizazz™: Pooh faces *(New)*
Solid Paper Pizazz™: light green, pink, blue *(Plain Pastels)*
Black pen: Zig® Writer by EK Success, Ltd.
Pens: yellow, blue, pink Milky Gel Roller by Pentel
Page Designer: Susan Cobb

Be Creative With Lettering

Journaling adds a personal touch to each page. The words provide information that the photos simply can't express! Make your journaling as magical as the photos with creative lettering.

Use templates, die cuts, stickers or Punch-Outs™. Or draw your own fancy letters in pen. There are lots of products available to help—these pages show how to use some of them!

Alphabet templates are an easy way to create fun journaling that can really make the page. The playful style of the letters mirror Piglet's and baby's expressions of youthful exuberance. Trace the letters onto patterned paper and cut just outside the drawn line—this black border helps make them stand out against any background.

Paper Pizazz™: Piglet paper (*New, Peek-a-Boo Pooh*), purple starburst (*Light Great Backgrounds*)
Solid Paper Pizazz™: white and dark pink (*Plain Pastels*)
Decorative scissors: Ripple by Fiskars®
Alphabet template: Wacky Alphabet by Frances Meyer, Inc.®
Purple pen: Zig® Writer
Page designer: LeNae Gerig

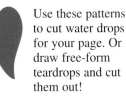

Use these patterns to cut water drops for your page. Or draw free-form teardrops and cut them out!

In this fun summer page Mickey appears to be juggling the photos! These swirly letters add to the water theme and are easier to draw than they look. They're free-form so you really can't make a mistake! Simply write the letters as you normally would and add a swirl to one end of each letter. When embellished with teardrop splashes this lettering looks all wet!

Paper Pizazz™: Mickey on stripes (*Mickey and Friends Peek-A-Boo*)
Solid Paper Pizazz™: blue, yellow (*Plain Pastels*)
Decorative scissors: Wave by Family Treasures™
Black pen: Zig® Writer by EK Success, Ltd.
Page designer: LeNae Gerig

Lettering doesn't have to be elaborate to be effective! Sometimes, a line at each letter-end is enough. Call extra attention to a single letter by using a template or die cut to make it. Use decorative scissors to cut a border strip and then embellish it with pen scallops and dots. The border provides a perfect place for journaling. Create an ABC scrapbook with an album page that features photos of activities for each letter in the alphabet!

Paper Pizazz™: Pooh and Piglet (*New, also available in bulk*), purple swirl (*Light Great Backgrounds*)
Solid Paper Pizazz™: lavender, dark pink, aqua blue (*Plain Pastels*)
Decorative scissors: Wave by Family Treasures™, Cascade Range Canyon Cutters by McGill Inc.
Alphabet Template: Classic Lower by Frances Meyer Inc.®
Black pen: Zig® Writer by EK Success, Ltd.
Page Designer: LeNae Gerig

This design perfectly illustrates how to fill a 12"x12" page when you only have a few photos of that theme. Plus it shows how creative you can get with letters! These large Goofy letters make excellent photo frames that fill the page and tell a bit about the day. Trace and cut out the letters (patterns on page 42). Trim the photos to fit behind the O's and glue to the page. Journal around the letters as shown and glue cutouts to interact with them. If you don't have actual photos of Goofy, try using photos of people acting "goofy!"

Paper Pizazz™: Goofy (*available in bulk*)
Solid Paper Pizazz™: white (*Plain Pastels*)
Cutouts: daydream Goofy, sitting Goofy, Goofy points (*New, Playtime with Mickey and Friends*)
Pens: black, orange Zig® Writer by EK Success, Ltd.
Page designer: Shauna Berglund-Immel

Include Memorabilia in Pocket Pages

Pocket pages are just a whole lot of fun to make and to look at! Pockets provide a handy place to include a bit of memorabilia with the page like an invitation or birthday card. Or, create a pocket and tuck a removable photo into it as shown below! Pocket pages are really simple to make, too!

Refer to page 11 to paper piece Kanga (patterns on page 44) taking care to glue her pouch only on three sides. Leave the top open to form a pocket. Silhouette-cut a photo and mat it on black. Slip the photo into the pocket and glue Kanga to the page as shown. Make a clever journal mat like the Roo one shown here. Cut the Roo face stamp from the upper left corner of the paper. Glue to a black square and triple mat it as shown. Journal on the square and glue it to cover the hole in the paper.

Paper Pizazz™: Pooh and friends face stamps (*New, School Days with Pooh*), peach moiré (*Pretty Papers, also available in bulk*)
Solid Paper Pizazz™: black, brown (*Solid Jewel Tones*), blue, white (*Plain Pastels*)
Black Pen: Zig® Writer by EK Success, Ltd.
White Pen: Milky Gel Roller by Pentel
Page designer: Shauna Berglund-Immel

This pocket page spread is very easy to make! Cut and mat three strips of Mickey silhouettes paper. Glue two on the photo page. Mat and glue a photo and Mickey Punch-Out™ as shown.
For the pocket: Use decorative scissors to trim the short edge of a 5"x8½" piece of black paper. Glue the paper to the bottom of a patterned sheet, leaving the top open for the pocket. Glue a matted patterned strip of paper that coordinates with the photo page to the front of the pocket. Add a bit of journaling and a Punch-Out™, then slip in special birthday cards.

Paper Pizazz™: Mickey Silhouette (*New, Playtime with Mickey and Friends*), red with white dots (*Ho Ho Ho!!!, also available in bulk*)
Solid Paper Pizazz: black (*Solid Jewel Tones*), goldenrod, red (*Plain Brights*)
Cards In Minutes™: Birthday Candles, Happy Birthday

Punch-Outs™: Mickey with balloons, Mickey stamp (*Mickey & Friends*)
Decorative scissors: Wave by Family Treasures™
White pen: Milky Gel Roller by Pentel
Page designer: LeNae Gerig

Make a "hunny pot" to store those sweet cards from your special event. It suits this baby shower theme well, but could easily fit another—imagine what Pooh's honey pot could hold if it were cut from brown paper and put on a Halloween background. Or cut from green and placed against a Christmas page! Simply trace the pot and label (pattern on page 47) onto the solid papers then cut them out. Cut a slit in the top of the pot. Glue the sides of the pot and the top rim edge to the background paper. Leave the center of the pot free of glue so that cards, photos, candy wrappers, or gift tags and wrap can slip in and out easily.

Paper Pizazz™: Pooh naptime (*New, Winnie the Pooh and Baby, Too!*)
Solid Paper Pizazz™: light and dark pink, yellow, light blue (*Plain Pastels*)
Cards In Minutes™: Rainbow Hearts, Pastel Quilt
Star punch: Marvy® Uchida
Knife: X-acto®
Alphabet template: Fat Caps by Frances Meyer, Inc.
Black pen: Zig® Millennium by EK Success, Ltd.
Page designer: LeNae Gerig

What a fun way to store your *Toy Story* autographs! This boot pocket could easily fit any western page theme, too! Trace and transfer the boot (patterns on page 45) to the paper and cut out. Cut the boot strap, spur and spur straps and mat each on black. Use the pen to outline the spur strap. Punch the spur circles and cut the boot sole. Glue all of the pieces to black paper and cut with a ⅛" border. Use the silver pen to outline the boot and to draw the details. Write "Autographs" to show what the boot holds. Punch four large stars and twenty ¼" circles from goldenrod. Glue a circle at each star tip for the sheriff stars.

Paper Pizazz™: Woody (*New, Toy Story*) crushed suede (*Black & White Photos, also available in bulk*) red tri-dots (*Dots, Checks, Plaids & Stripes*), metallic silver (*Metallic Papers*)
Solid Paper Pizazz™: black (*Solid Jewel Tones*), blue, goldenrod (*Solid Bright Papers*)
Cutout: Woody star (*New, Toy Story Punch-Outs™*)
Large star, ¼" circle punches: McGill, Inc.
Small circle punch: Marvy® Uchida
Brown pen: Zig® Chisel and Fine tip by EK Success, Ltd.
Silver pen: Hybrid Gel Roller by Pentel
Page designer: Susan Cobb

27

Create Peek-a-Boo Pages

This technique creates a mini-album in your scrapbook! Peek-a-Boo pages are a series of three or four pages, with a shape cut from the paper that makes a window revealing something on the next page. It links many pages to one theme so you can create a photo journal of the day's events. Cut a window in your scrapbook page to feature one photo throughout the whole story. As each page is turned, more photos are revealed, but the most magical picture is still visible!

page 1

page 2

Choose a background paper that will work on all pages. Decide where and what shape the Peek-a-Boo window will be, then cut it from the page.

This example uses pink background sheets with one sheet of *Sleeping Beauty* patterned paper cut into strips for a border on all four pages. An oval window is cut from page two and three. When turned, the window reveals the focal photo on page one and page four. Other photos of the event are cropped and matted then glued in the available spaces throughout the spread.

The technique on pages 16-17 help re-create the flower near Princess Aurora in the patterned paper. Punch three hearts and group them points outward as shown. Glue a circle punch for flower centers. Creative line art also links the decorative elements to the patterned paper.

Paper Pizazz™: Sleeping Beauty (*New, Disney Classics*)

Solid Paper Pizazz™: light and dark pink, yellow, lavender, light and medium blue (*Plain Pastels*)

Cutouts: Fauna, Flora, Meriwether (*New*)

Decorative scissors: Jumbo Lacy Scallop by Family Treasures™

Heart and circle punches: Marvy® Uchida

Pens: Black, purple, light and dark blue, green Zig® Writer by EK Success, Ltd.

Gold pen: Hybrid Gel Roller by Pentel

Page designer: LeNae Gerig

page 3

page 4

This three page Peek-a-Boo photo journal captures the magic of Disneyland in the shape of a balloon die cut! In this example, the shape is cut from a corner of the first page and used to crop the photo on the last page to peek through it (die cut patterns on page 45). Page two (below, left) is designed on the back of page one. Mat other photos to fill the spaces. Use patterned and solid papers to mat, carrying the same colors throughout the spread. The frolicking Punch-Outs™ that decorate the inside pages reinforce how excited and happy everyone was to be there! This spread illustrates great use of the Mickey balloon patterned paper. It's used as page corners on each page and continues the balloon theme throughout the pages. The smaller balloon die cut shapes also connect the pages as well as the similar pen work used to border each photo and page.

page 1

Paper Pizazz™: Mickey with balloons *(New, Pairs of Mickey)*

Solid Paper Pizazz™: aqua blue, red, goldenrod *(Solid Bright Papers)*, black *(Solid Jewel Tones)*

Punch-Outs™: Donald with pencil, Mickey with balloons, dancing Mickey, dancing Daisy, Pluto, headstand Goofy, skipping Minnie, Mickey signature, Pluto signature *(Mickey and Friends)*

Balloon Die Cuts: Accu/Cut® Systems

Decorative scissors: Ripply by McGill, Inc.

Pens: black, red Zig® Writer by EK Success, Ltd.

White pen: Milky Gel Roller by Pentel

Page designer: LeNae Gerig

page 2

page 3

Design Flaps, Doors & Windows

Add an element of surprise by including a door or window that actually opens to reveal a photo, message or plain fun! Almost any shape can be made into a door or window as long as it has a hinge.

Cut a red piece of paper to 10"x6½" and fold it in half widthwise. Glue a 5"x6½" piece of goldenrod inside the back flap. Glue four ¼"x6½" green strips to cover the edges. Trim each strip end at an angle so they don't overlap. Cut and fold three ¼"x¾" goldenrod rectangles in half lengthwise. Glue over the crease on the door front as shown for hinges. Glue the door to a 5½"x7" piece of blue paper. Draw two door panels and embellish each with punched stars and journaling. Punch a small circle and two ¼" circles and glue as shown for the doorknob. Mat Mickey and friends cutouts. Glue them inside the door, overlapping as shown with Goofy's and Donald's bodies extending from behind the green trim. Embellish it with star punches.

Paper Pizazz™: Mickey & Friends faces (*New, also available in bulk*)
Solid Paper Pizazz™: red, blue, green, goldenrod (*Plain Brights*)
Cutouts: Mickey, Minnie, Goofy, Donald, Pluto (*New, Playtime with Mickey and Friends*)
Small star punch: Family Treasures™
Small circle and ¼" circle punches: McGill, Inc.
Black pen: Zig® Writer by EK Success, Ltd.
Page designer: Susan Cobb

For the card flaps: Mat two playing cards and two photos on black paper and cut to 2⅝"x3¾". Cut four foot-hinge pieces (patterns on page 42) from black and hinge two black rectangles together. Trace and cut out four red hands and feet. Draw the detail lines. Mat each piece on black. Glue to the cards as shown. Open each card and journal in the empty spaces. Embellish with heart punches. **For the faces**: Trace and transfer the large heart to red and the inside heart to pink. Cut out and mat each on black. Glue as shown. Trace, transfer and glue the nose and mouth hearts to the pink heart face. Use black and white pens to draw the eyes and outline the facial features.

For the croquet wicket card: Trace and transfer the bending card pattern to white and pink. Cut out, mat and glue as shown. Punch a red heart and glue as shown. Glue a face, feet, arms and hands to the card as shown. Draw the details.

Paper Pizazz™: Alice in Wonderland (*New, Disney Classics #2*)
Solid Paper Pizazz™: black (*Solid Jewel Tones*), pink, white (*Solid Pastel Papers*) red (*Plain Brights*)
Small and medium heart punches: Family Treasures™
Decorative scissors: Cork Screw by Fiskars®
Pens: white, orange Milky Gel Roller by Pentel
Black pen: Zig® Writer by EK Success, Ltd.
Page designer: Shauna Berglund-Immel

This easy treasure chest is so versatile, it could fit any theme depending on the card, patterned papers and photos you choose! Turn a patterned *Cards In Minutes™* so the fold is at the top (or cut a piece of patterned paper to 6½"x8¾"). Open it up and lay it flat, white side up. Fold the bottom 3¾" up and crease. Fold the remaining top flap over to close it.

If desired, mat it before folding the chest. Glue the blank side of the card to a black sheet and cut out with a ⅛" border. Use coins patterned paper to line the inside of the chest. Glue it to the black paper and trim the edges even. Then fold it as directed above. Embellish the chest with Punch-Outs™, cutouts, paper strips and pen work. Mat a photo and journal banner (pattern on page 41) to include inside the chest.

Pull the stern wheel element from the background paper (discussed on page16-17) to make a photo frame that matches the patterned paper perfectly! Crop a photo into a circle and mat it on black. Glue it to brown paper and cut out with a ¼" border. Use a black pen to draw rope lines. Punch out teardrops and diamonds, mat on black and glue to the wheel as shown.

Paper Pizazz™: Pan characters (*New, Disney Classics #2*), coins (*Book of Firsts*)
Solid Paper Pizazz™: black, brown (*Solid Jewel Tones*), neon green (*Plain Brights*), white (*Plain Pastels*)
Cutouts: gold corners, gold lock (*Embellishments*)
Teardrop and diamond punches: Family Treasures™
Banner die cut: Ellison® Craft & Design; **Gold pen:** Hybrid Gel Roller by Pentel
Black pen: Zig® Writer by EK Success. Ltd.; **White pen:** Milky Gel Roller by Pentel
Page designer: Shauna Berglund-Immel

Trace and transfer the patterns to the paper colors indicated on page 48. Cut two ⅞"x1⅝" vellum pieces and glue for window panes. Glue the blue turret pieces behind the turret windows. Arrange the pieces on the background paper as shown. Glue the turrets in place. Silhouette-cut a photo to fit in the upper window. Glue it in place, then glue the upper castle portion to the page. Slip a Cinderella cutout under the main castle piece so she is looking through the small window. Punch two holes and a medium heart in the draw bridge as shown. Tie the ribbon pieces to the draw bridge then insert into the castle and tie to secure. Journal on the inside draw bridge surface. Crop a photo so it shows through the draw bridge opening and glue it in place on the page. Glue the castle piece over it. Punch seven small pink hearts and glue to the castle pieces. Outline the castle details with a black pen. Color in the pink details with a pink pen.

Paper Pizazz™: green tiles, cobblestone (*Textured Papers*), clouds (*Vacation, also available in bulk*), barnwood (*Country, also available in bulk*), vellum (*Vellum Papers*)
Solid Paper Pizazz™: dusty blue (*Solid Muted Colors*), pink (*Plain Pastels*)
Cutouts: Cinderella, Jaq and Gus dancing (*New*)
Small and medium heart punches: Family Treasurers™
⅛" hole punch: McGill, Inc.; **⅛" wide pink satin ribbon:** two 9" lengths
Knife: X-acto®; **Black pen:** Zig® Writer by EK Success, Ltd.
Pens: pink, blue and white Milky Gel Roller by Pentel
Page designer: Shauna Berglund-Immel

Make Magically Moveable Parts

Playing with a scrapbook page is almost as much fun as finding a pot full of honey! These pages invite hands-on play as viewers pull, turn and slide parts of each page looking at the photos and movement!

Slip the page in a sheet protector and slit the plastic as needed to move the parts while the page remains protected.

Pull-tab pages have always been irresistibly inviting—and easy to make, too! Cut one 2"x11", one 2½"x11" one 1"x11" and one ½"x2" strip of green paper. Tape the 2"x11" strip flush with the left side of the page. Cut a ¼"x8" slit in the center of the 2½"x11" strip and trim the right long edge for a patterned border. Glue the 1"x11" strip to a 1"x11" cardstock strip for a stronger pull tab. Wrap the ½"x2" strip around the pull tab as shown in the diagram for base tabs. Use tape to secure. Slip the 2½"x11" border strip over the pull tab so the base strips are showing. Tape the matted Tigger to the base tabs. Write "Pull" at the top of the pull tab. Embellish the border strip with pen work as shown. Mat photos and cut a journal star (pattern on page 43). Cut around Tigger's ear and paw to slip two photo edges underneath as shown.

Paper Pizazz™: peeking Tigger (*New, Peek-a-Boo Pooh*)
Solid Paper Pizazz™: green, yellow, blue (*Plain Pastels*)
Punch-Outs™: Tigger bouncing on tail (*Pooh*)
Star die cut: Accu/Cut® Systems; **Déjà Views ruler:** by C-Thru
1"x11" strip of white cardstock
Decorative scissors: Wave by Family Treasures™
Black pen: Zig® Writer by EK Success, Ltd.
Page designer: LeNae Gerig

base tab diagram:
flaps extend over the border strip.
Glue Punch-Out™ to tab face.

The wheels on the page go round and round! Trace a 7½" circle onto white paper and cut out with decorative scissors. Repeat for a 7" circle using Piglet paper. Cut a 2½" wide circle ⅜" down from the top of the Piglet circle. Mat on pink paper with a ⅛" border. Cut a circle ¹⁄₁₆" smaller through the pink paper so the circle is "matted", too. Cut four photos into 3" circles and glue one at 12:00, 3:00, 6:00 and 9:00. Glue a Piglet Punch-Out™ between each photo. Glue to the center of the tri-dot paper. Place the Piglet circle over the white circle and insert the brad in the center. The Piglet circle will turn to reveal each photo! Embellish the wheel and page corners with letters, patterned corners and another Piglet Punch-Out™.

Paper Pizazz™: fall leaves Piglet (*New*), tri-dots on pink (*Light Great Backgrounds*)
Solid Paper Pizazz™: pink, white (*Plain Pastels*)
Punch-Outs™: posing Piglets (*Pooh*)
Decorative scissors: Wave by Family Treasurers™; **½" long brass brad**
Alphabet template: Classic Caps and Classic Lower by Frances Meyer, Inc.®
Dark pink pen: Zig® Writer by EK Success, Ltd.; **Knife:** X-acto®
Page designer: LeNae Gerig

Pooh always waves an eager "Hello" to all who hold his paw! Trace and transfer Pooh onto goldenrod and his shirt onto red. Cut out the pieces and glue Pooh's shirt onto him, and his sleeve onto his arm. Insert the brad through the sleeve and body as indicated on the pattern. Bend back the prongs to secure. Trace and cut the flag from the papers shown. Journal on it and glue the flag into Pooh's moveable paw. (Pooh's body and flag patterns are shown on page 39.)

Paper Pizazz™: Pooh's favorite things *(New)*
Solid Paper Pizazz™: goldenrod, red *(Plain Brights)*, pink, lavender *(Plain Pastels)*, black *(Solid Jewel Tones)*
⅛" wide circle punch: by McGill, Inc.
½" long brass brad
Black pen: Zig® Writer by EK Success, Ltd.
Page designer: LeNae Gerig

Mickey is such an active little Mouse, you know he loves this water slide! Cut the right edge of a 5½"x7½" white sheet of paper at an angle with Wave scissors to curve like a slide as shown. Keeping the wave edge free of glue, glue it to a dark blue sheet and cut ½" away following the same slide curve. Repeat for light blue and white as shown—vary the wave widths if desired. Cut a ¹⁄₁₆" wide slit the length of the slide in the light blue wave to follow the curve. Glue the slide on the page. Mat the Mickey cutout on cardstock. Attach a ⅛"x¾" piece of foam tape to extend ½" behind Mickey as shown in the small photo below. Wrap the exposed paper clip with light blue paper and secure it to the back of Mickey with tape. Insert the extending paper clip into the water slide slit and see how smoothly Mickey slides!

Paper Pizazz™: surfing Mickey *(New, Playtime with Mickey and Friends)*
Solid Paper Pizazz™: white, dark blue, light blue *(Plain Pastels)*, goldenrod *(Plain Brights)*
Punch-Outs™: swimming Pluto *(Mickey and Friends)*
Cutout: sliding Mickey *(New)*
4" square of white card stock; Foam mounting tape;
Paper clip; Clear tape; Knife: X-acto®
Decorative scissors: Wave by Fiskars®
Pens: black, blue Zig® Writer by EK Success, Ltd.
Page designer: Susan Cobb

Perfectly Paper Pieced Disney Characters

If you can trace, you can paper piece! Piecing Disney characters together allows you to bring unique texture and originality to your pages. You can dress characters according to your page theme and color scheme. No one else will have a page like yours!

Best of all, you gain a warm satisfaction from having done it yourself! Step-by-step instructions are provided on page 11 so you can refer back for help at any time!

Minnie's got a whole new wardrobe based on the paper choices you make! Trace the patterns for Minnie Mouse on page 41 and follow the general directions on page 11 to piece her together. Punch nine small flowers from solid papers. Outline each with the black pen and glue an ⅛" goldenrod punched circle for centers. Glue onto Minnie's shoes, in her hair and around her neck as shown. Mat three photos to place on the page. Cut the top long edge of a 2" wide strip of grass paper with decorative scissors for a page bottom border. Journal and embellish with more brightly colored flowers.

Paper Pizazz™: water *(Vacation #2)*, grass *(Pets, also available in bulk)*
Solid Paper Pizazz™: green, fuchsia, orange, blue, goldenrod *(Plain Brights)*, white *(Plain Pastels)*, black *(Solid Jewel Tones)*, peach *(Solid Muted Colors)*
Decorative Scissors: Mini Pinking and Mini Scallop by Fiskars®
Small flower punch: Family Treasures™
⅛" circle punch: McGill, Inc.
White pen: Milky Gel Roller by Pentel; **Black pen:** Zig® Writer by EK Success, Ltd.
Page designer: Susan Cobb

Trace the patterns for Mickey Mouse on page 40 and follow the general directions on page 11 to piece him together. Trace and transfer the cupcake wrapper and candle patterns from this page and the yellow mouse head from page 40 and cut them from the papers you've chosen. Crimp the cupcake wrapper in a paper crimper. Trim the long sides of a ¼"x1" blue strip with Mini Scallop scissors for a candle and punch a teardrop for the candle flame. Trace and transfer the blue mouse head pattern on page 40. Mat it and use it for a journal area.

Paper Pizazz™: Mickey silhouette on red *(New)*, colorful dots, cork board *(School Days, also available in bulk)*, red pinstripe *(Dots, Checks, Plaids & Stripes, also available in bulk)*
Solid Paper Pizazz™: black *(Solid Jewel Tones)*, peach *(Solid Muted Colors)*, blue, green, red, goldenrod *(Plain Brights)*
Teardrop punch: Family Treasures™
Paper Crimper: by Marvy® Uchida
Decorative Scissors: Mini Scallop by Fiskars®
White pen: Milky Gel Roller by Pentel
Pens: black, red Zig® Writer by EK Success, Ltd.
Page Designer: Susan Cobb

Trace the patterns for bedtime Goofy on page 42 and follow the general directions on page 11 for piecing him together. Trace and transfer the blue mouse head pattern on page 40. Mat it and glue it to the page. Glue Goofy to overlap the shape and journal in the ears around Goofy's body.

Paper Pizazz™: blue Mickey tiles *(New)*, red and white stripes *(Ho Ho Ho!!!, also available in bulk)*
Solid Paper Pizazz™: red *(Plain Brights)*, white *(Plain Pastels)*, black *(Solid Jewel Tones)*, peach *(Solid Muted Colors)*
Black pen: Zig® Writer by EK Success, Ltd.
White pen: Milky Gel Roller by Pentel
Page Designer: Susan Cobb

Piecing Pinocchio takes a bit of time—that's no lie. But the dapper little wooden boy is very well worth it! Trace the patterns for Pinocchio on page 43 and follow the general directions on page 11 to piece him together. Cut two strips of three Pinocchio tiles patterned paper diamonds and glue to the page top and bottom for a border. Cut one diamond, mat it and glue it as a "cutout". Use the star pattern above to cut and mat a journal area, then add line work to embellish the elements, too!

Paper Pizazz™: Pinocchio tiles *(New, Disney Classics #2)*, dots on purple *(Child's Play, also available in bulk)*, dots on yellow *(Light Great Backgrounds, also available in bulk)*, red pinstripe *(Dots, Checks, Plaids & Stripes, also available in bulk)*
Solid Paper Pizazz™: red, aqua blue, goldenrod *(Plain Brights)*, black, brown *(Solid Jewel Tones)*, peach *(Solid Muted Colors)*, white *(Plain Pastels)*
Decorative scissors: Mini Pinking by Fiskars®
Black pen: Zig® Writer by EK Success, Ltd.
Pens: white, pink, light blue Milky Gel Roller by Pentel
Small star punch: Family Treasurers™
¹⁄₁₆" circle punch: McGill, Inc.
Page designer: Susan Cobb

What a perfect frame for this photo! Coordinate the pattern with an element of the patterned paper or one in the photo—or both! Crop your photo in an oval shape and mat it on green paper. Trace and transfer the leaf pattern below to goldenrod and green papers. Cut out enough leaves to surround your oval size. Use the pen to draw detail lines on the petals and around the flower center. Glue a few green leaves to extend from around the sunflower center first—just as they are in the patterned paper. Then glue the goldenrod leaves overlapping them. Journal along the page border and with matted template letters on the patterned paper.

Paper Pizazz™: sunflower Pooh (*New, Pooh On the Edge*)
Solid Paper Pizazz™: blue, green (*Solid Pastel Papers*), goldenrod (*Solid Bright Papers*)
Green pen: Milky Gel Roller by Pentel
Black pen: Zig® Writer by EK Success, Ltd.
Alphabet Template: Déjà Views™ by C-Thru®
Page designer: Shauna Berglund-Immel

The carriage door could easily be made into a door that opens to reveal the entire photo inside. Simply double mat the door on yellow paper and glue a small rectangle for a hinge. Trace the blue carriage pattern pieces on page 46 and cut them out of the papers shown. Glue them onto yellow paper spaced ⅛" apart as shown here and cut out with a ⅛" border. Trace the yellow pieces and cut them out. Trace the door patterns and door oval. Crop a photo so it fits inside the door window. Glue the door pieces over the photo as shown. Transfer the detail lines and use the silver pen to draw over them.

Paper Pizazz™: Cinderella (*New, Disney Classics*), blue stars (*Birthday Time!, also available in bulk*)
Solid Paper Pizazz™: pink, blue, yellow (*Solid Pastel Papers*)
Silver pen: Hybrid Gel Roller by Pentel
Blue pen: Zig® Writer by EK Success, Ltd.
Small star punch: Family Treasures™
Decorative scissors: Mini Scallop by Fiskars®
Page designer: Susan Cobb

Tinker Bell could easily be outfitted in different clothes to match your page theme. Just as Minnie Mouse donned a luau outfit for her trip to Hawaii (shown on page 32), Tink could wear a blue starburst dress for a Fourth of July page. Or a denim dress for a teen page! She could even wear a pastel patterned dress for a baby-themed page.

Trace Tinker Bell's pattern on page 43. Transfer the master pattern onto peach paper. Transfer and cut her hair from yellow and the dress and shoes from a pattern that matches your page theme. Use the circle punch to make two white tassels and glue to the shoes. Outline each piece with black pen. Assemble Tinker Bell as shown. Cut wings from vellum and glue to her back. Use the pens to draw her detail lines and to color in her bow, eyes and mouth.

Embossing is easy! Use the embossing pen to write or draw as you would with any pen. Sprinkle embossing powder over the drawn lines. Return excess powder to the jar and heat the ink with the heat gun until the powder is melted.

Paper Pizazz™: starry night *(available only in bulk)*, vellum *(Vellum Papers)*
Solid Paper Pizazz™: peach, yellow, white, green *(Plain Pastels)*, silver *(Metallic Papers)*
Pens: light blue, white, salmon Milky Gel Roller by Pentel
Silver pen: Hybrid Gel Roller by Pentel
Black pen: Zig® Millennium by EK Success, Ltd.
Embossing pen: Duo Embossing Pen by All Night Media® Inc.
Silver embossing powder: by Embossing Arts
Heat gun: by All Night Media®. Inc.
¼" circle punch: McGill, Inc.
Page designer: Shauna Berglund-Immel

Use this die cut shape for a journal area on the page below and on the Tigger page on page 32.

star die cut © & ™ Accu/Cut® Systems

Trace the patterns for Tigger on page 47 and follow the general directions on page 11 to piece Tigger together. Cut the Pooh Christmas paper into strips and glue to a sheet of blue paper leaving a 4½" wide strip empty for Tigger to be placed on. Glue Tigger to the page and draw the tree lights wire to wrap around him in a tangle. Use the oval punch to make orange, red, yellow and green lights. Glue along the wire.

Paper Pizazz™: Pooh Christmas *(New, Special Days with Pooh)*
Solid Paper Pizazz™: orange, green, red *(Plain Brights)*, yellow, pink *(Plain Pastels)*, black *(Solid Jewel Tones)*
Star punch: Family Treasures™
Small oval punch: McGill, Inc.
Star die cut: Accu/Cut® Systems
Decorative Scissors: Mini Scallop by Fiskars®
Pens: black, red Zig® Writer by EK Success, Ltd.
Page designer: Susan Cobb

Dress Up Die Cuts

Put a new twist on an old pattern and make your die cut shapes unique! Die cuts can easily be cut apart and pieced together to make a multi-colored, multi-patterned decorative element that's all your own. It's fun to dress up a die cut to resemble the people, colors or elements in your photos or background papers. And it's as easy as strolling through the Hundred-Acre Wood!

Trace the doll shape (pattern on page 45) on the back of patterned or colored paper. Draw around the doll ⅛" larger than the traced doll shape. Then cut below the neck and above the elbows and knees to create shirts, dresses, pants and shorts! Use the original shape as a base, and go from there! Make a hat or hair, cut socks and shoes, or gloves and coats! Use colored pens to draw details on the faces and clothing.

Paper Pizazz™: Mickey paper (*New, Pairs of Mickey*), rainbow Mickey (*New, Playtime with Mickey and Friends*), white with red dots (*Ho Ho Ho!!!, also available in bulk*)
Solid Paper Pizazz™: goldenrod, red (*Plain Brights*), black (*Solid Jewel Tones*), white, peach (*Plain Pastels*)
Paper doll die cut: Accu/Cut® Systems
Small and medium circle punches: Family Treasures™
Pens: black, brown Zig® Writer by EK Success, Ltd.
White pen: Milky Gel Roller by Pentel
Page designer: LeNae Gerig

Add color to a die cut! Cut the car from the papers indicated on the pattern on page 43 and follow the general directions on page 11 to piece it together. Cut away the center of the windshied and insert a photo. To fill the car with friends, simply silhouette-cut each picture and glue them to extend above the car. Journal on the license plate and draw an "MM" for a Mickey hood ornament.

Paper Pizazz™: Toon Town (*New, Magic Kingdom*)
Solid Paper Pizazz™: red, goldenrod (*Plain Brights*), black (*Solid Jewel Tones*), white (*Plain Pastels*), silver (*Heavy Metal Papers*)
Car die cut: Ellison® Craft & Design
Black pen: Zig® Millennium by EK Success, Ltd.
Silver pen: Hybrid Gel Roller by Pentel
Knife: X-acto®
Page designer: Shauna Berglund-Immel

Pooh patterns for page 33. Cut the body, arm, shirt and flag from the colors shown.

Icon patterns for page 23.

Insert brad here to secure arm.

Mirror pattern for page 12. Cut the pieces from the colors shown.

Pooh pumpkin for page 15.

pumpkin die cut © & ™ by Accu/Cut® Systems

39

Mickey's hand pattern for page 17. Cut two and turn one over for the right hand.

Mickey head patterns. Pink for page 19, blue for pages 34 and 35, yellow for page 34.

Fold tracing paper in half. Place fold along dashed line.

Mickey paper piecing patterns for page 34.

40

Minnie paper piecing
patterns for page 34.

Tub and towel pattern for page 23.

Banner pattern for page 31.

banner die cut
© & ™ by
Ellison® Craft
& Design

41

G-O-O-F-Y for page 25.
Cut two letter Os.

Bedtime Goofy paper piecing
patterns for page 35.

Croquet Wicket Card for
page 30. Hand, foot and
hinge patterns for page 30.

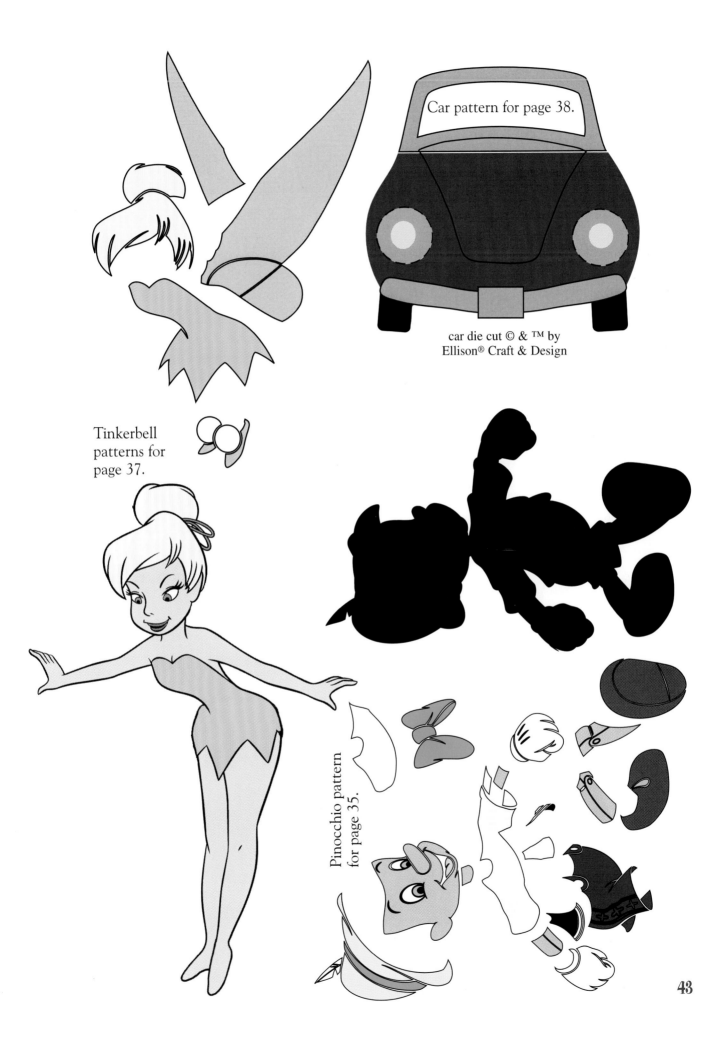

Car pattern for page 38.

car die cut © & ™ by
Ellison® Craft & Design

Tinkerbell
patterns for
page 37.

Pinocchio pattern
for page 35.

Kanga patterns for page 26. Cut the pieces from the paper colors shown.

Mouse ears balloons patterns for page 29.

balloon die cuts © & ™ by Accu/Cut® Systems

paper doll cut © & ™ by Accu/Cut® Systems

Paper doll pattern and clothes for page 38.

Woody's boot for page 27. Cut the patterns from the paper colors shown.

Cinderella's carriage pattern for page 36. Cut the pieces from the paper colors shown.

Hunny pot pattern
for page 27.

Cut here to slip
keepsake cards
into pot.

Fold tracing paper in half. Place fold along dashed line.
Trace a pink label and glue to the pot as shown.

Tigger patterns for page 37.
Cut Tigger from the paper
colors shown. Use the pen
to add his black stripes.

Castle patterns for page 31. Cut each piece from the papers shown. Use the pink pen to color in the pink details as shown. Cut the gray window panes from the upper window and glue vellum behind the openings.

© Disney

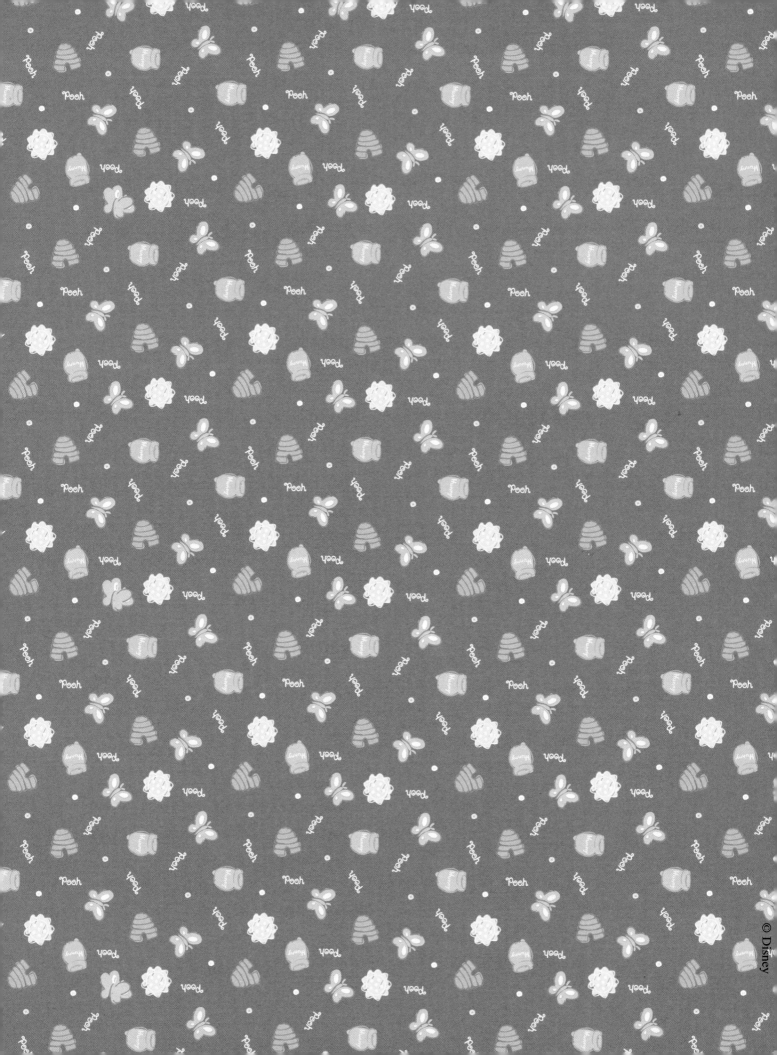

 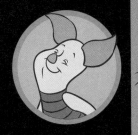   

   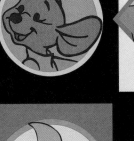  

© Disney

little friends deserve big hugs, little fluttering friends, butterflies and bees, buzz, buzz, buzz, wandering in the wood, toe tickling grass, flower scents tickle your nose, little friends deserve big hugs, little fluttering friends, butterflies and bees, buzz, buzz, buzz, wandering in the wood, toe tickling grass, flower scents tickle your nose,

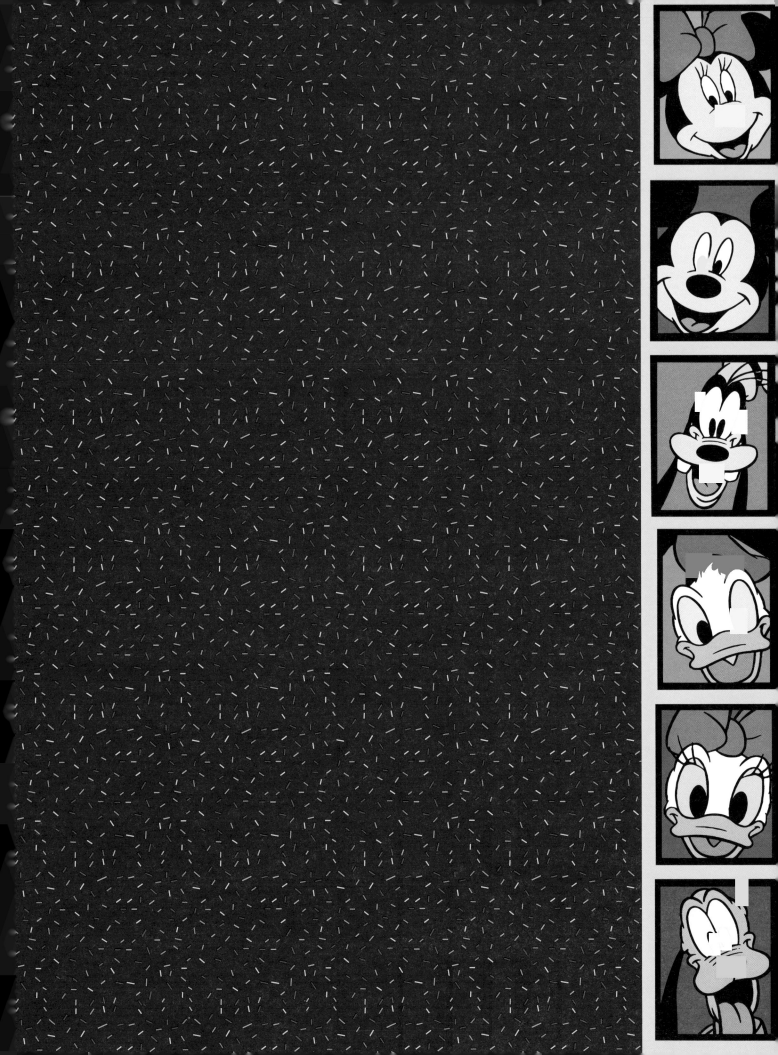

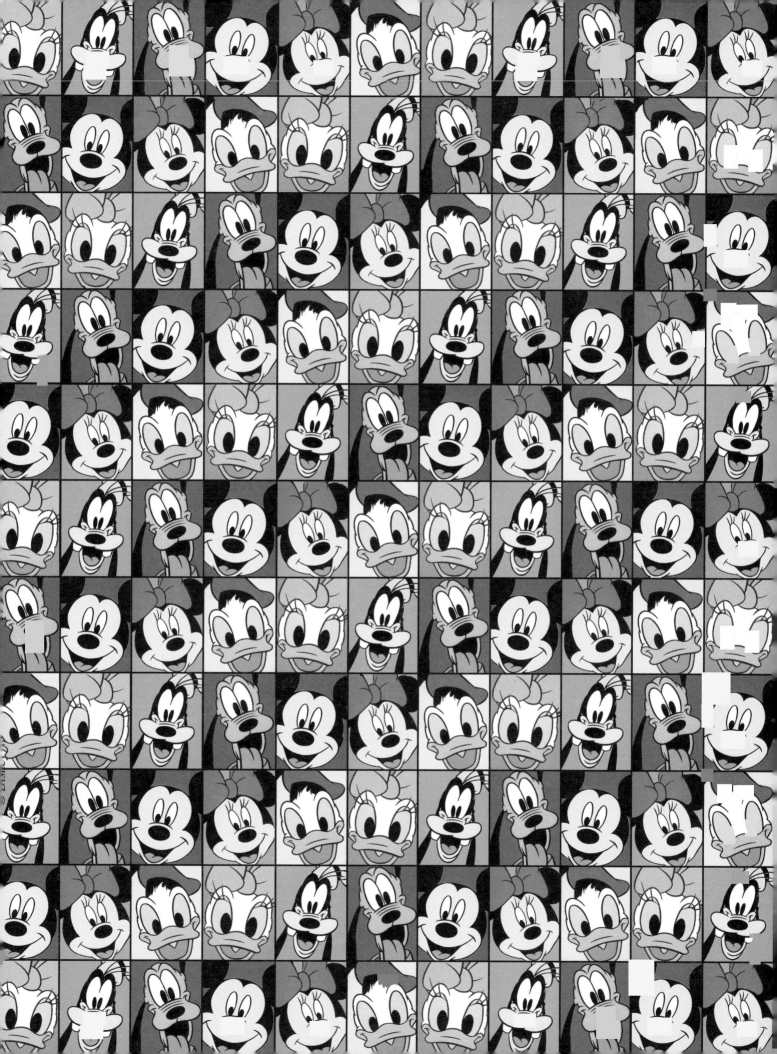

MICKEY

MOUSE

© Disney

© Disney

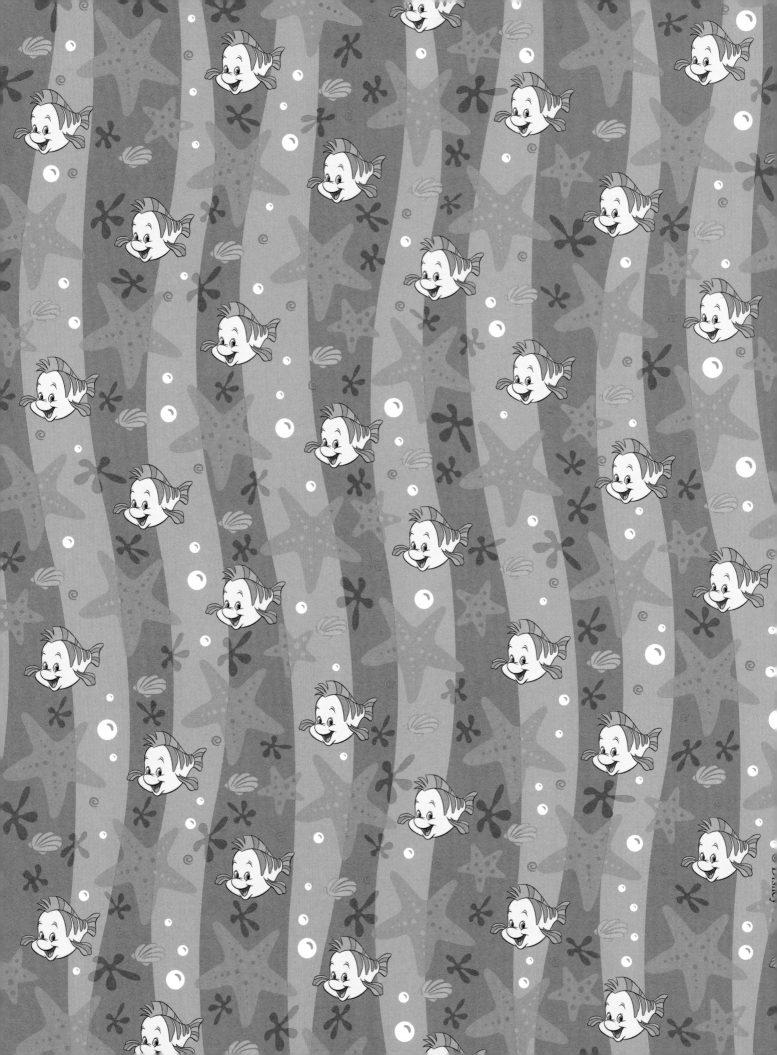

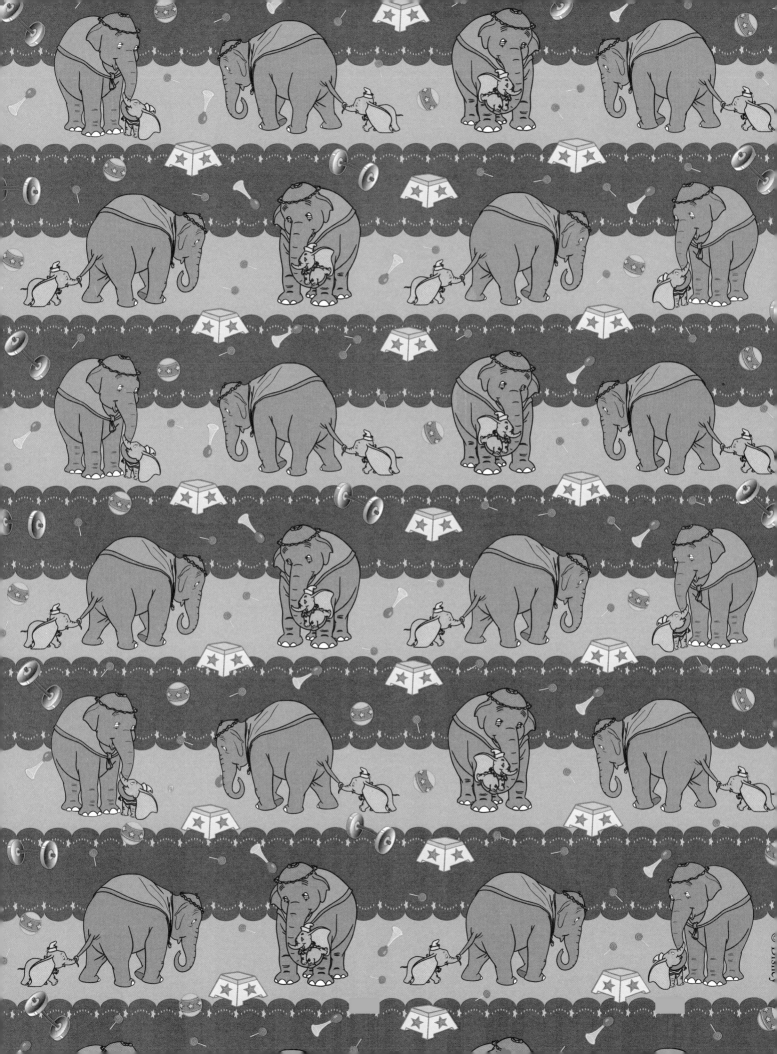

© Disney
© Disney
© Disney
© Disney
© Disney
© Disney
© Disney
© Disney
© Disney

© Disney